was @ ?
Bonnie's?

Dream Stanzas

An Anthology of Poetry

By Julie Longstreet Wehmeyer

©2022

Joanne,

Namaste,

Julie

Longstreet

Wehmeyer

Dedications and Thanks.

I would like to thank my girls, Chloe, Hilary, Morgan and Caridwen for giving my life purpose and reason. You are the biggest blessings in my life. I love all of you to the moon and back.

I also would like to thank, my inspiration and love of my eternity James/aka as Cosmo. I am holding you to the promise of meeting me on the Banks of the River Jordan when it is time for you to bring me home. I know you are relishing your freedom from pain and using your new wings as you soar through the heavens like you used to dive in the ocean. F*ck cancer.

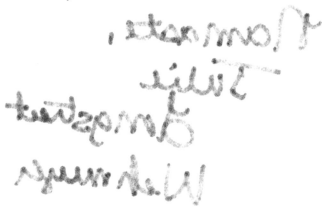

Table of Contents

L'Appel du vide
The Call of the Void

The overwhelming yearning for the beckoning inky
darkness
Of absolute nothingness
Of blackness
Of never-ending loneliness
Where all physical sensations are gone
Except hollowness and emptiness
Steeped in a darkness so pervasive that even
Shadows run away in apprehension and fear
Where all light is banned and forsaken
And where
There is no sensation of physical touch
No feeling in the body
Except for the brain and the
Brain works overtime generating
Emotions, feelings, and thoughts
Such dark, dangerous thoughts
Such beautiful, glorious, and delicious thoughts
It is over. It is done. We are finished. Good bye.
So go on step in front of that train,
While listening to the whistle scream
"Move away, move away, move away."
As the light coming toward you is blinding you to
reality you really do not want
Or simply arch your back and spread your beautiful

White feathered wings as you step off the ledge of a
building or bridge and soar through
As you watch the ground summoning you with its
Inevitable bone-crushing, soul-stealing last blow
But it is just a momentary desire to fall into the void of
nothingness
You know you will not follow through,
And you take a step back,
Yet the desire and fear are real and palpable
The urge to live is so much stronger than the need for
darkness.
But for a moment, a brief short moment of insanity,
The temptation for falling into nothingness is
Such a strong almost impossible urge to end.
L'Appel due vide
The Call of the Void

Oneness

I crave the oneness
Which has nothing to do
With being alone
Reaching across the veil
And through the mists of time
Through millions of years
Two hearts beating as one
Two sets of lungs breathing as one
Four eyes seeing as one
Two souls dreaming and loving
And forgiving as one
Two must become one
And I crave that oneness
And the love so deep
That I ran from in fear and youth
And suddenly, you are here
In ways that I never expected
Unexpectedly, gratefully, joyously
My heart soars in recognition that
We are one.
We are one.
We are love.

Morning Desire

Like a teenage virgin with my first true love,
I gently caress you and breathe in your essence.
Holding you firmly in my hands, and
Passionately drinking you in while
Relishing your delicious, deep, dark, sensuous heat.
I ravenously devour your heart, soul, and spirit
Not stopping until your vessel is empty and dry as
bone.
Then without a moment of hesitation...
I will guiltlessly, and with
No second thoughts, regrets nor remorse
Walk away from you, leave you, and
Gleefully cheat on you in wild abandonment
With your beautiful, hot, luscious, brother
My Second Cup of Morning Coffee

Sad State of Affairs

It's quiet tonight in this airport
Neither one of us has much to say
Soon it will be time for you to get on board
The plane which will take you away
You're holding my hand so tightly
I know you don't want to go
But there's someone across the country
Who's waiting for you to come home
It's a sad, sad state of affairs we are in
We should have known better than to let it begin
Cause now we know it must come to an end
This sad, sad state of affairs
This sad, sad state of affairs

Now the time has come for you to depart
You kiss me and tell me to smile
You say someday soon we'll be one again
Until then, we'll just have to get by
Those words seem so easy for you to say
Can't you see how they tear me apart?
Every time you board another plane,
Can't you see that you're breaking my heart?
This sad, sad state of affairs
This sad, sad state of affairs

I Could Not Speak

When I was a child,
I could not speak because only adult thoughts mattered.
When I was a teen,
I could not speak because authority figures had to be
respected.
When I was a worker,
I could not speak because my knowledge was
threatening.
When I was a wife,
I could not speak because my opinions were
inconsequential.
Now, as an old woman,
I cannot speak, because I do not exist.
I lurk behind my smile and my perfectly made-up face
and coiffed hair.
I must be pleasant.
I must not speak.
I do not exist. I never have existed.

Really?

So, the universe has decided '
That you are my "one."
For eternity.
Why?
Is this my truth?
I did not ask for this.
Maybe you did not either.
Do I even have a choice?
Does it matter if I thought I did?
Another one loves you.
So very very much.
So why do you keep coming for me?
Again, and again, and again.
Like a mantra repeating itself.
I don't want to hurt anyone.
Yet, I crave the sacred closeness when you hold me.
I love the peace my heart feels with you.
Please.
God.
Help me do what is right for everyone.
Is there an answer?
Is this heaven or hell?

The Aloki

In the never-ending darkness,
Surrounded by so many other transitioning souls,
I saw you there
Emanating heat, love and light
Tall, majestic, and incredibly strong
Your arms, or were they wings?
Were outstretched toward me
You are not the Angel of Darkness
You are the Angel of True Light.
The welcoming radiance in the
Darkness that I was drawn to
"Come home, child" you said.
And I walked to you and
You wrapped your golden white wings with golden tips
around me
In such a warm caring embrace.
So warm, so safe, so loving.
My mortal pain was gone, as
I melted into your embrace.
You took me to a home
I had remembered only in my dreams
From a time long ago.
I thought you would be frightening.
I thought I would be terrified.
That you'd be wearing a black robe and carrying a
scythe
I thought you would be fearsome
But you just love

And you love me
You are light and love, warmth, and beauty
Why was I so scared of you?
I did not dissolve into nothingness, and I did not
disappear.
My soul and spirit is forever.
You are not a demon, there is no hell
There is only warmth, light, love, guidance, and
forgiveness
Wrapped in the arms of my Aloki –
My Savior, The Angel of Death

14 Broken Angels

14 Broken Angels
Are crying in the back garden.
Their hearts and hopes and dreams shattered and
crushed
And laying in the grass like rubble.
As salty tears are running in rivulets
Down their hard stony cheeks
While the demons laugh in the distance down the long
alley of darkness.
Cheering like champions after a hard-earned win
Mocking our human ignorance, intolerance, and
foolishness
That we self-righteously clasp to our chests
Like a dowager clutching her pearls at Sunday morning
mass
Thinking her prayers will solve everything.
Not wanting to get her hands dirty
While 14 broken angels cried in the back garden
Thunder from the Divine could be heard
Crashing in the distance with a deafening roar
Burning and brimming with
An anger at hot as lava
Spewing from the broken
Heart of our precious Earth
Seeming to shout in frustration
"Just how broken must your
souls be before you wake up?"

14 Broken Angels
Are crying in the back garden
Their hearts and hopes and dreams shattered and
crushed
And laying in the grass like rubble.

There You Are

"There you are." My soul sung out when I saw you for
the first time
As if it had been looking for you for a lifetime.
And it had been looking for you for so long
At a funky little Irish pub in Cambridge, Massachusetts
in 1987
Smack dab in the middle of Porter Square
It felt like the Keith Whitley song
"Ten Feet Away"
And I thought to myself…
"Lord, why is this good old boy looking at me like that?"
Like I was "his."
And my brain answered, "Julie, that ain't no boy. **That's
a man.**"
"Oh shit."
"I married the wrong one."
I never ever thought of you in any terms,
but we were meant to be married.
And I knew somewhere in some dimension in some
other lifetime
We would be
Because we always had been
I had been yours for eternity.
You looked like a big old working man from Tennessee
Ten years and a generation older than me with
seemingly nothing in common.
I could smell whiskey and cigarettes coming off you
from ten feet away

And you thought I was a child, yet so grateful I was a
woman
Long scruffy blond hair combed back like some kind of
baddass Conway Twitty,
Trying so hard to look like an outlaw
Rough, scratchy sideburns snaking down your jawline,
You were like a caricature
Of what a Nashville badboy should look like,
But that just was not you at all
And I wanted to kiss those sideburns.
And breathe in that whiskey cigarette male scent of you
And eventually I did
Just not that night.
Your black sleeveless t-shirt stretched tightly across
your chest
A massive broad chest chiseled from years of high
school and college football.
You were a force to be reckoned with
Chunky turquoise bolo tie casually draped around your
neck
Don't you know, you do not wear a bolo tie with a t-
shirt?
But the look worked on you.
Only you could pull that off
Baggy white running pants and beat up old tan working
boots
Oh, I thought you were not my type.
Even though my soul and DNA screamed out otherwise
I was used to bloodless, passionless Harvard boys.
But male heat rolled off you like waves of volcanic lava

Promising a love that would be impossible to describe
Or resist (how could I resist?)
And I sat there like a snotty little waspy
Boston girl who thought she was too good for you
Like I had done so many lifetimes before...
I was in so much trouble
But this was fate, this was a gift from the Divine
It would not and could not be stopped.
The Universe set this in motion millions of years ago.
I was yours and you were mine,
We were "us." and we have always been "us."
I refused to look back you at you, but could feel
Your fiery blue eyes bore into me
Flaring and burning like the center of a flame
Not cool, aloof, and calm, like you would think the color
blue would be
But with such intense heat I could feel it on my skin
Straight through to my soul
Your eyes implored me as if to say, "yes, here I am and
there you are."
"Now, what are we going to do?"
And with all the arrogance I could muster,
I finally stared back at you, and flashed my sad little
wedding rings at you
And grasped my husband's arm possessively
Like he was all I ever would need and
As if to say, "I am with him!"
A boy who would never grow up to be a man or a good
Daddy
Something you just instinctively knew

How to be and deep in your soul wanted to be.
But you gave up those dreams and desires out of
misplaced male pride
Yours eyes got big and a bit angry as you rolled them
"You silly little girl. See if I care."
"Do you really think those cheap little gold rings you
are shoving in my face
Could ever deter me? Would ever even deter me?"
HA! you mocked me
But you did care, didn't you?
You cared so much and never stopped.
You cared and loved like a man, not a boy.
It was something I had never experienced before.
But you were more than I could handle at that time.
A young mother of two daughters, barely 27 years old
And even though I ran like little fool,
When I should have stayed and faced my fate
Forcing the Universe to take us by the hand
In a most unexpected way
Five years later to make things right.
I did not run then.
Could not run then.
And you always knew,
You never gave up.
You never gave up.
You never gave up.
There you are. My soul sung out.
That is the one.

I Loved You Most

And, when the strength you found in the bottle
Brought out the affectionate side of you,
You would hug and hold me so close, while
Wrapping me in your deceptive warmth.
I didn't care that you were drinking.

And, when you would howl out her name
In unbearable, heart-wrenching agony,
Unable to raise your broken body and soul
Off the cold tiled bathroom floor.
I didn't care that you were drinking.

And, when you looked at me confused and
Unable to even recognize my face because of
The ferocious hunger you felt to bring her back
While your grief was swallowing you whole.
I didn't care that you were drinking.

Because, when the lights at night were dimmed,
And you thought she was the one lying next you,
You would reach out and tenderly hold me tight,
Loving my body with such rapture, that
I didn't care that you were drinking.

I loved you most when you were drunk.

Mother Always Said

When I asked her why she never said?
"I love you," to me,
My mother always replied,
"Actions speak louder than words,"
So, she never complimented me,
Never told me I was pretty,
Never told me I was smart.
She never hugged me spontaneously,
And always refused to hold my hand.
But the sadistic glee in her eyes and
The joy in the smile twitching on her lips
When she pummeled with slaps and fists
After pulling me out of bed
Screaming in uncontrolled rage
In the middle of the night
For normal childish mistakes and misdeeds
Made it abundantly clear,
That if nothing else
My mother was an honest woman.
For her…
"Actions spoke louder than words."
Do you want to see the scars?

Bill

Your tiny infant bones are
Buried in the middle of Austin.
Somewhere. I don't know where.
Our father took me there once
To show me your gravestone.
It only said "Son."
It took them over twenty-two years
To mark your final sleeping place.
They used my college money
To buy the stone I begged for you.
Mother laughed when she told me
Your tombstone was my graduation gift.

And,
I hated you for dying
And leaving me alone with them.

You were the first.
Born three years, five months,
And six days before me.
Breech birth complications
Strangled you to death with
The cord that kept you
Alive for nine months.

Mother said you were stillborn
But you held on for three long days.
They never named you.
They never baptized you.
They never honored your tiny life.

And,
I hated you for dying and
Leaving me alone with them.

Mother said they were going
To name you Henry William III
After our father.
You were to be called Bill,
But they didn't want to waste the name
On a dead baby.
When they might have another son
To be third in line.
Instead, I came along and was
Named after our grandmother.
They despised me and resented
That I needed them to care for me.

And,
I hated you for dying,
And leaving me alone with them.

I fantasized that we would be
Best friends and buddies.
Dreaming you would be my protector,

My cherished, obnoxious, older brother.
My knight in shining honor.
I imagined we would help each other
Through the shared nightmare of them.
We would nurse each other's bruises
And shame from the neglect
Of not being wanted or loved.
Instead, you abandoned me
Before you even knew me.

And,
I hated you for dying
And leaving me alone with them.

You escaped.
And I survived.
I love you.

We Are Being Played

So many flames have been extinguished and
Deprived of crucial life-giving oxygen
While denying Mother Earth of vital
Human heat, warmth, and love.
Mankind's raging rivers of ignorance,
Intolerance and arrogance
Drown everything with its demanding, unquenchable,
Impatient thirst.
But soon there will be a roaring howl of anger
Emanating from deep within the bowels of this planet
We call home.
A fury that will be felt vibrating and throbbing
Within the veins of our lost souls
As we try to grapple with the consequences coming due.
And the demons, they mock us and laugh at us
All the while pretending to be angels.
Or maybe they are just angels
Being angels.
Trying to show us how we have gone wrong?
Yet our seething mortal pride and ego keep our eyes,
And our hearts, tightly closed.
We are just human fools.
We are being played.
Wake up.
Wake up.
Wake up.

Lola Ann

Three husbands.
Three sons.
Three grandsons.

Born in 1943, Lola Ann was always
The dutiful homemaker and wife.
She never became the free love spirit
She so yearned and wanted to be.
Now time is running out on her,
Like the pages in the notebooks
She spent her lifetime filling with poems
Spewing her childish dreams
Thoughts, feelings, and emotions.
Dreams never maturing beyond the ruminations
Of a lonely teenaged girl filled with angst.
Lola Ann, oh Lola Ann.

Three husbands.
Three sons.
Three grandsons.

She surrounded herself with men.
Earning her own self worth
By constantly trying to please them.
Reflecting their aspirations and wants
Into a mosaic molded to fit her needs.
Their dreams and accomplishments

Became her misguided desires in the dark shadows of
them.
Lola Ann willingly gave up the womanly sacredness
That was God's precious gift to her.
She could not let herself surrender,
Breathe deep and calm her own mind.
Lola Ann, oh Lola Ann.

Three husbands.
Three sons.
Three grandsons.

The husbands are all gone now.
Two sit in urns on her mantle
And one cavorts in younger fresh pastures.
Sitting alone in her house on the hill,
She lives a fantasy life in the books she devours.
In the home that has become a prison
Due to self-indulgence and self-neglect.
There is no man or friend to catch her
When she falls and cracks her head open
On the beautiful Mexican tiles
In the kitchen she so cherishes.
Lola Ann, oh Lola Ann.

Three husbands.
Three sons.
Three grandsons.

Suddenly too tired to reach for her phone
As blood pools around
Her closely cropped white hair.
Hair that once was vibrant, sleek, and black
Attracting husbands to her with its mysterious luster.
Lola Ann's deep brown eyes are starting to fade
As the blood continues to flow
Like toxic grief from her wounds,
Emptying her veins onto the floor.
Her heart slows with regret.
She finally surrenders.
Lola Ann, oh Lola Ann.

Three husbands.
Three sons.
Three grandsons.
Lola Ann, oh Lola Ann.

Grimes County Beauty

Just a couple of hundred fence posts
Separated Henry from Emma growing up
In Grimes County, Texas in 1915.
Coming from good old first-generation German stock
Staunch Lutherans and followers of The Truth.
Ten months older and a hundred twenty pounds
heavier than her,
Emma never ever stood a chance with Henry.
With flaming, red curly hair, and bright blue eyes
And a singing voice like a flock of golden cheeked
warblers,
Emma was the local beauty and dream of many.

But they said it was God's will
She got what she deserved
God's will for being so damn beautiful.
God's will for being young and naïve.
It did not matter that it was against her will,
It was God's will, they said.
And against her will, her fate was sealed.

Seventeen-year-old girls can be so foolish.
And Emma was no different in this way.
And Henry was raised to think "like a man,"
Womenfolk were God's gift to Men
For pleasure and homemaking and sometimes
degradation.
Emma flirted with and unleased a demon.

And when Henry decided the time was right,
He raped her into motherhood, marriage
And the never-ending contempt of the good people
Of small-town, Navasota, Texas in 1915.

But they said it was God's will
She got what she deserved
God's will for being so damn beautiful.
God's will for being young and naïve.
It did not matter that it was against her will,
It was God's will, they said.
And against her will, her fate was sealed.
They said it was God's will.

When her belly started to grow,
A shotgun wedding was quickly planned
Not a white dress wedding filled with joy for Emma,
The good people forced her to her knees, and through
tears
Made her confess her wanton, lustful sins to them.
After begging forgiveness from the pious Lutheran folk,
These stalwarts of decency finally let Emma take her
vows
While they slapped smug-faced Henry on the back
Praising him for being such a man
For winning the Grimes County beauty of 1915.

But they said it was God's will
She got what she deserved
God's will for being so damn beautiful.

God's will for being young and naïve.
It did not matter that it was against her will,
It was God's will, they said.
And against her will, her fate was sealed.

One More Night

The last light of life had started to flicker
Deep in your dark blue eyes
That held so many secrets, mysteries, and love.
Desperate to slow down the inevitable,
I curled up next to you on that hard white hospital bed.
Listening to the beeping sounds all around us
Feeling every breath, you tried to breathe.
My hand on your chest willing your tired and weary
heart
To just keep going.
Please just keep going.
And I prayed.
I prayed so damn hard.
The prayers became a mantra.

Live…Live…Live…Live…Live…

I lit candles and incense.
And I prayed even more.
With such ferocity and desperation,
I made promises to God
That never would be kept, that never could be kept.
Please God, give his pain to me.

Take me…Take me…Take me…Take me…Take me

Just give me one more day.
One more tender hard sweet kiss.

One more beautiful night of his arms
Wrapped tightly around me.
Loving each other.

Please...Please...Please...Please...Please
One more day.

I Dove

I dove.
I dove again.
And again.
And again.

I could not leave you where they left you.
Your soul struggling for salvation
Deep in those dark, unholy, black waters
So close to hell. So close to hell.
Your body bloating and disintegrating
Into the louring seabed below.
I dove and dove, reaching and grasping to find you.
Until my hands finally touched your skin.
And I brought you home.

I dove.
I dove again.
And again.
And again.

My strong, calloused hands found and brought you
home.
The life and love gone from your amber eyes
The eyes I lovingly and passionately dove into every
night.
Seaweed all tangled up in your golden red hair.
Your lips once warm and moist with honey
Were now cold, blue, and briny from the sea.

I lifted you up and carried you back home.
Back home hidden deep in the dark recesses
Of the sanctified holy ground
They tried to deny you because of our sin.

I dove.
I dove again.
And again.
And again.

My mother's childhood rosary beads
Wrapped and entwined in your fingers.
Your body wrapped in the blanket we loved so hard
beneath
I prayed and covered you with the sacred promise of
love.
As I dove into the neve ending hot lava river of grief
Disguised as a small glass flask in my back pocket.
I deeply gulped and sank into its smoky oblivion
Knowing it was all that would sustain my soul
Until God brings us back together again.

I dove.
I dove again.
And again.
And again.
And again.

The Harlot

The desperate howl
Of my lover's keening
Vibrated in the water around me.
As my husband held my head down in the sea
Growling under his breath,
"You are mine."
"You are mine."
"You are mine."
Precious clear air quickly being
Replaced by murky filthy water in my lungs
As I struggled and fought to live.
To live, and to love.
To love just one more time.
"Harlot" they shouted.
"Witch" they chanted.
A celebration of hatred.
An army of men held my lover back
Held my true love back.
Pinning his arms down,
Keeping him from me,
Forcing him to watch me die.
Breaking him, destroying him
As he struggled to save me.
To protect me.
To stop the madness.
To keep loving me.
This was our punishment for love.
I shuddered and died.

And with every cell in my body
I cursed my husband.
I promised to return.
I became the witch.
I was the harlot.

In a Perfect World

A minute was all it took, and I knew
I had made too many promises too soon
I never knew you were waiting for me
The way my heart had always waited for you
A minute was all it took, and I knew
I am paying a debt that will always be due
I never will get away, never will be free
From the promises I once vowed to keep
In a perfect world, we would be together
We would never ever have to say good-bye
We could mean it when we said forever.
It would be a perfect world, just you and me.
But a minute was all it took, and I knew
We would never see this love come true
We will never be all that we could be
Our perfect world will only be in our dreams.

I Never Wish Upon the Right Star

Lying here alone in the grass
I stare up at the sky
Hoping I can find a lucky star
Wishing you were still mine
But there will never be enough stars
To bring your love back to me
No matter how many may fall
My heart will never be free
I will never wish upon the right star
Or find a good luck charm
That will ease the aching in my heart
I will never wish upon the right star
I have worn myself out asking
What did I do to make you leave?
But daylight is almost here
It is time to set your memory free
I never will

We Don't Love Here Anymore

My suitcase is in the hallway
And my clothes are packed inside
There's a U-haul in the driveway
So now it is time to say good-bye
The house feels so empty
There's not even a rug on the floor
Baby, can you tell me just why
We don't love here anymore.
t looks like we don't love here anymore
And we never will again
The love that we once shared
Somehow, we let come to an end
I thought this home would be ours forever
But today we are closing the door
On all the dreams we've left here
We don't love here anymore
I remember the good times spent on this porch
The memories were just so beautiful then
But now, there's a "for sale" sign out front
We won't ever love here again

Don't Ask Me to Lie for You

The news that you just told me,
Is hard for me to take.
You confess that you've been cheating
So, what do you want me to say?
Because I stood up for you when you married
And I heard you take your vows
But now, I'm standing up for him this time
So don't ask me to lie for you now.
I won't lie for you
I won't be your alibi
I won't be on your side
I won't be a part of your breaking his heart
I won't lie for you
Don't even expect me to
Our friendship goes back a long way
And I've always told you the truth
But my conscience won't let me play this game
So don't ask me to lie for you.

I Will Never Marry You

I never will marry you, no matter how long we are
together
Although neither of us know that now.
And even though I may end up loving you dearly
I never will trust or love you enough to share my name
with you.

Our attraction was instantaneous, passionate and fiery
But shameful and embarrassing at the same time
You were so willing to quickly drop everything that
should have truly mattered to you for me
Without a thought or concern
And without any sense or care about who you were
hurting.
You abandoned a husband of 15 years and two precious
little boys
You made me feel sorry for you, like you such a victim
of his neglect
In time I will see that you were not a victim, but in fact
you victimized and manipulated others
Including me
For your own needs and desires
A play that you will perform repeatedly through the
years.
It is always, always, always about you.
Those boys never will recover from
the model of love and devotion you have presented to
them.

That Mommies leave when the going gets tough
without care or concern.
That it is okay to leave with no remorse nor looking
back and the chaos you caused.
What you fantasize is a magical fairy tale romance, true
love,
Claiming that our souls touched, and we were destined
for each other
Is really nothing more than lust and selfishness on both
of our parts.
Although neither of us can see it that way right now.
And you convinced me in the beginning that this
fantasy was real,
But this is not the kind of love to build forever on.
Seven years younger than you,
I will end up giving up my youth and dreams of a
family for you.
You already fulfilled those dreams for yourself,
And out of selfishness and self-centeredness you have
denied them from me.
But I was in too deep before I realized all I lost.
And I accept responsibility for that,
But I will always regret disappointing my family and
myself.
For what we have done
Adultery is never something to glorify with words like
"soulmate" "fated" and "sacred."
I may not leave you, but it will be more out of guilt,
pride, and inertia and to

Show others and myself that I made the right decision
with you
Even though you will show repeatedly
Just how selfish and willing you are to hurt others.
So, I never will marry you, no matter how long we are
together.
Although neither of us know that now.
And even though I may end up loving you dearly.
I never will trust you or love you enough to share my
name with you.

Dominic

Dominic is 94 years old,
Pale, Frail and oh so fragile
He sits for hours on the stoop
Of his apartment building
On 84th Street in Bensonhurst
His kind Jamaican caretaker beside him
Watching and caring over him.
As he watches the pretty girls walking by
Occasionally waving, always smiling, always smiling
Dominic spent a lifetime walking, working,
Loving and living in the Brooklyn neighborhood
Where he was born
His Sicilian immigrant parents taught him to be a good
man
Be nice to the ladies, they said
Be kind to the old ones
Kiss the babies
Go to Mass
Find a good girl and get married
And now Dominic sits in the hot sun
Outside of his apartment building
A flock of biddies from other apartments
Line up along the stoop next to him
As they have done for decades
Sitting in their folding chairs and lawn chairs
They tire him with their gossiping and nastiness
Life is too short for that he has always thought
So, he watches the girls

And they rush by, fancy coffees in their hands
And he smiles to himself,
They don't even know what good espresso really is
Not the way a good Sicilian gentleman knows
Carrying their shopping bags in their hands
Rushing home to husbands and boyfriends
Reminding him of all the girls he kissed
And loved in this old borough
And suddenly there she is, the single mom with the two little boys
Who lives in Apartment 2C
He always wonders where the man is
She should not be alone
She always smells so nice
And stops to say hello and touch his hand
And he struggles to get up like a good gentleman should
He's embarrassed to be sitting down in front of a lady
He forces himself up and reaches for her grocery bags
Insisting on taking them to her apartment
The caretaker and the mom let him take her bags
While they help him go into the building
Holding his elbows firmly to keep him upright
And to protect his pride and dignity
Dominic carries the groceries inside
No woman should carry bags!
Not while he still can.
And he smiles to himself,
Feeling like he is 35 again.
Taking deep breaths to smell her beautiful perfume

Cherishing the feeling of her arm wrapped under his
And his eyes start to water slightly
As he pretends, he is bringing her home after shopping
And that she will go inside, and she will make him and
the boys
Sunday dinner and love only him
And that he will play with the little boys, teaching them
how to
Be good men like his father did.
In another lifetime, she would have been his
In another lifetime, she will.

Feathers

Startled awake from what felt
Like a deep, endless slumber,
I felt you caressing my feet.
Your delicate hands as soft and cool
As the finest satin.
Like I remembered them to be.
Lady's hands that never toiled.
How can this be?
I buried you myself
In hidden sacred ground
More than 30 years ago.
Yet, now, here you are.
Where have you been?
Why are you here?
Where am I?
I asked those questions
But my lips never moved or quivered.
You knew and answered me with your heart
And smiled with such love and kindness.
My heart clenched and surged in my chest as
I doubled over in relief
And so much love.
"Darling, it's time. It's time to fly home."
My arms, shoulders and back were tingling
As my skin had started to rip and tear
In tiny straight lines.
In a zig zag jagged pattern.
Tiny white tendrils were emerging through.

Feathers.
There was no pain
Just a tremendous sense of relief
Of coming home.
And a surge of strength
Enveloped in warm feelings
Of being blanketed in love.
My weak old body felt so strong …
Stronger than it had in decades.
I'm growing wings.
Feathers turning golden at the tips.
My mortal life was through.
My tired flesh and bones
Were no longer needed.
Life was over.
Devoid of me.
Yet my spirit was bursting
Full of love and freedom
And you.
I am empty and full
At the same time.
I just want to fly.
I want to fly home.
I want to fly home with you.
Our wings wrapped around each other.
My hot gold against your cool silver.
Diving and soaring
Through the stars and the Universe.
As we have done through eternity.
We are finally together.

We Saw Each Other

You reached up and gently,
But firmly grasped my arm
As you guided me down from the steed.
The way you had done many times before
Keeping me safe, cared for
And protected.
A young lady and her family's groom
From very different worlds and expectations.
For the first time, I looked down
And saw your face.
I saw your face.
I saw you.
Instead of looking through you
With the unearned arrogance
I foolishly considered my birthright.
I truly, and finally, saw you.
Your eyes as deep, blue, and dangerous as the waters
At the base of Aillte an Mhothair.
The desire to leap into their watery depths
Was overwhelming, instantaneous, and fierce.
I should have recoiled
Holding my head high and proud.
I should have dismissed you and walked away
As society demanded a I do.
Yet seemingly, with no other choice,
I let myself tumble and fall over the precipice
Into the dark mysterious danger of you.
The danger of us.

Without any resistance.
Without any remorse.
And you saw me too.
For the first time
You truly saw me.
As no one else in this ever had or could.
Recognizing the brokenness
Mirrored in the blackness of our separateness
That only served to make us one.
Igniting a flame deep within our spirits,
A flame that has burned for many lifetimes
Both of us
Willingly, and without fear,
Accepted the challenge that our souls demanded.
Never once flinching in reticence
As the boundaries of our lives were obliterated
We were damned.
We were blessed.
We saw each other.

Enough

As a child, I was always told what I was not
Never what I was.
You are not smart enough
You are not pretty enough
You are not thin enough
You are not clever enough
You are not loveable enough
You are not wanted enough
I simply was not enough of anything
So, now when I look in the mirror
And try to see my own reality
I am overwhelmed by feelings of
Delusion and confusion
And I wonder
Am I who or what I think I am?
Do I exist outside of the paradigm of my parent's
design?
Or am I just an illusion created to placate their feelings
Of inferiority and insecurity?
Will I ever be enough?
For anyone
For myself?
Will I ever be enough for anything?
Or am I simply a broken unfixable work in progress?

Sacred Lions

We are only living in these human frames
As spirit souls encased in
Flesh, bone, blood, and muscles
Until we wear out these suits of limitation
And give them up
To the saving grace of mother earth
We will stumble along swallowed up by
Our hubris and arrogance
Defining ourselves by self-assigned adjectives
That do not exist and are meaningless
Forgetting that we are all simply
I am…
I am…
I am…
We are all sacred lions swimming
Against the current of the deep
Dark and deadly rivers
Where there are no adjectives.
No expectations.
No ego
Only I am…
I surrender my will because
I simply am…
I am.

Orbs

Lying next to you in our bed
And the feelings are so strong
The attraction is so full of intentional power and desire
That we find yourselves joining together in the ancient
Sacred dance as old as time
That brings us as close as two beings can
Be in mortal flesh
And we find our souls suddenly exploding
And shattering into millions of tiny
Atomic sized orbs of light, bliss, and joy
That scatter throughout the room and out into the
Universe
And we must lie still, oh so still,
While holding each other so tight
And with such love and beauty,
We wait for the orbs to coalesce and come back
To us so you can breathe and move again
And when they return,
They are so drenched in love and passion
And have mixed and joined together
With the orbs of both of us
We truly become one with All.
Our DNA is altered forever.
We are different; we are no longer singular.
This is love.
This is sacred.
This is oneness.

Santiago and Lily

Booking it like a madman down I-10,
Pulling a full load from El Paso to Houston
A message pops up on Santiago's phone
"Call Mom, there's been an accident."
And with heart stopping instant reflexes,
Santiago pulls his rig over and calls.
"Lily's been hurt, get home as fast as you can."
Was all he heard
Lily, his brand new 28-year-old bride of two years
Santiago's foot hit the metal and
He was flying low on the straight desert road
toward Houston and home.
Lily … Hit and run by a distracted driver
While walking the dog
Then left on the side of the road
To die like roadkill
Her body broken, bloodied and shattered in so
many pieces,
Lily was holding the angels at bay as best as she
could
Waiting for Santiago
But time was running out
And the miles between them seemed never ending
and endless

Santiago arrived in time to crawl into the
emergency room bed with Lily
It was too late to do anything but say good-bye
HIs soul and heart shattered by the emptiness
That was impossible to process
And he held her broken body in his arms, covered
her with love
Kissed her gently one last time and let her slip
away
Never given the chance to have children, Santiago
and Lily thought they had forever, and they should
have
So Santiago now travels the nation's roads in his rig
With their three cats who keep him connected
And sometimes at night before he falls asleep
He feels feathers caressing him
And running up and down his arms
And the goosebumps rise where he was touched
And he knows she is there and waiting for him
Waiting to bring him home
Where he wants to be more than anything.
So now he is just biding time.
So grateful for those feathery touches
As se clutches her pillow to his chest and cries.
And cries.
And cries.
And prays for more goosebumps.

Your Home

There have been so many places
Through the years that I've called home
Just places where I've hung my hat,
Until I got the urge to roam
Now, I've finally found my piece of heaven,
That I can call my home
I know I will stay forever
As long as I've got you to hold
Your home is where my heart is,
The only place I want to be
I only feel at home whenever you are with me
The love you have given me, is all I will ever need
Your home is where my heart is,
And that's where I want to be.
The only place I want to be.
There will be storms to ride out
When the winds of change blow
Baby, you can rest assured,
You won't ride them out alone
I'm ready to put down my roots,
There's no more need for me to roam
This home is on solid ground,
Where the love we share can grow.

How Much Love Can This Heart Hold?

How much love can this heart possibly hold?
How much passion can this body endure?
I have cried for you, and died for you.
I have wanted you, and exalted you.
How much love can this heart possibly hold.
I've wanted and loved you for millions of years
Never truly believing I'd ever hold you near
The wanting and desire for you bringing me to tears
Now the reality of my dreams is finally here
I never dreamed our love would be like this
The ecstasy filling my soul with such bliss
These feelings for you have me falling over the precipice
I never thought God would give me a life so blessed.

About the Author

First published nationally at age 14, Julie has racked up numerous writing awards. She has been published in several anthologies, Cat Fancy Magazine, Playgirl, Readers Digest and other publications. Julie was a Professional Songwriter scholarship recipient at Berklee College of Music in Boston, MA. and has won numerous lyric writing awards.

She lives the life of a nomad, traveling the country visiting friends, giving readings and making new friends in her 28-foot motorhome. In her spare time, she enjoys photography, making jewelry, soap and reading.

www.writinitdown.net